Her Inner Depths

Emily Mellentine

Presentation by *BookLeaf Publishing*

Web: www.bookleafpub.com

E-mail: info@bookleafpub.com

ISBN: 9789357612890

First edition 2022

DEDICATION

Dedicated to my younger self and my little
sister, Sophia.

PREFACE

Her Inner Depths, my first book, was completed right after my 21st birthday. This personal creation consists of poems about intimate and profound emotions, getting through rough times due to mental illness, suicidal ideations, and sexual assault, and learning to live independently. Writing has always been one of my most considerable coping skills to keep me on this earth. Ever since I was a young girl, crying down the halls in school, I found my place pen down in a journal. This book means more than the weight of the words on the paper; it serves as an emblem that, in the depths of darkness, you, too, can find the light.

Phases (1)

As a woman
tied to the moon
which rules the tides
I find comfort in her waves
accepting both her calming foam
gently reaching for the shore
and her thrashing depths
that few dare to dive into

-e.m.

Cinderella (2)

What stops a soul from searching
what suspends her in her fear
stalling the hands on the clock
from striking her destiny?

Could it be
her calendar, too full
her person, too pleasing
her bed, too comfy
their grip, not warm enough
in the midst
of running toward her destination
on a path not yet made clear

-e.m.

Golden Frame (3)

From my closet I choose
silk pants
a pressed blouse off its hanger
I paint my face with overpriced product
curl my hair to a crisp
put my jewelry on
and slip on my heels

I put so much effort
into one thing I can control
you look at me
see my polished in a poised body
see the thought behind my eyes
you don't see
but maybe
maybe you can feel...

my nervous energy
my self-doubt
my internal war
my criticisms and judgments
my mural I paint for you to see
the multicolor palate made of desperation and
despair

a golden frame encapsulating a messy truth
a brush avoiding a wrong stroke
details spent hours on to distract
from a mistake, an error, a blemish
a hole punched in the canvas skin
sewn back up with a shiny thread
that never seems to end

-e.m.

Honey Eyes (4)

5

You can not see it, can you?
Not when your honey eyes
see only through your point of view
Here, look through mine
Now you can see
the way your smile lights up my dark rooms
the way your curls lay down your back
the way the ink in your skin protrudes
I love you
I always do
imagine a life where we see the truth
to see all the good
that is you

-e.m.

Women (5)

Would you like to burn me at the stake
for all that I am
for my femininity
you praise and condemn simultaneously?

Would you like to keep me tied up
held down
hidden away
from my encompassing truth?

Would you like to extinguish
my will
my power
the natural fire that burns inside me
keeping me alive?

My heartbeat will drum on
no matter how hard you try!
This is the fight
that we are trying to survive

-e.m.

Sophia (6)

I love her
like the sun loves the moon
I love her
as my own
how she will love herself someday soon

I love her
as the tides love the shore
I love her
as so I hold the stars to her eyes above my own
for she will always mean so much more

-e.m.

I am here for you, forever and always, honey (7)

I see myself in her
in her struggles
in her faults
I want nothing more than to save her
but how does one save a child from their adult?

For they could not see how deeply she hurts
her scars not quite yet healed
but I
I know
how she truly feels

The dreaded hours spent worrying
as she walks down the halls
she can't seem to find herself
honey, there is no hurry at all

One day you will be free
one day you will feel peace
until then
honey, you have to stay here with me

-e.m.

Doe-eyed Hyperawareness
(8)

In every fiber of my being
awareness flows through
the world does not turn
without my witness
eyes do not pass
to form a glance
but a universe away
a long, slow stare
for how does one meet my eyes
and decide to look away

-e.m.

How lonely am I (9)

As I lie in a bathtub
drowning under the warmth of city water
as if it were a human hug
How desperate am I
to feel the excitement and pleasure
as their look into my eyes
deepens past a glance
How crazed am I
creating storylines of what could be
obsessing over fantasies
How hopeless romantic of me
to imagine a reality
where I am loved

-e.m.

Everything at once (10)

I often run until I crawl
and crawl until
I can do nothing but collapse to the ground
looking up at the hill of obligations before me
how can something feel so daunting and
overwhelming
yet empty and boring
at the same time
how do I reach contentment
when I fall back and forth between
feeling nothing at all
and everything all at once

-e.m.

The loneliness in me sees the loneliness in you (11)

I'd never known how a few words could ground
me as so
until I read the words
"you know I'm here for you"
my spinning inner world slowed down and at
once
I felt recognition
that while I'm holding my shoulders back
drowning in the sea of opportunities I'm clinging
onto
control and impulsivity reigning high
fighting for every fleeting moment of having it
all together
I feel recognized
as someone who needs someone to be there for
them
I type back, "and I'm here for you"

-e.m.

Not Enough, Not Enough
(12)

It's just not enough
to fall short of perfection
It's just not enough
to make an attempt at all

What do I do this for?
why every evening
do I end up on the floor
in a discontent state
of painful existentialism
garnished by mania and false thoughts
all I want is more, more, more

I want to scream
don't leave me, comfort me
please be here for me, hold me
as I construct a metal wall around myself
stuck between all that I want
and all that I'm too scared to have

It's just not enough
to live in my body
I confess
It's just not enough

to be in my mind

I hope you do not
relate and understand
for you are full
and it is truly just I
that is not enough

-e.m.

Seeing Red (13)

Passing roadsigns and stoplights
restaurants and bare trees
driving blurry eyes and a weightless body
to the next spot
where I can sit
and resist the hellish present
in which I live

-e.m.

To fly (14)

Sitting on my windowsill in the dead of night
with the permanent forever lasting knowledge
that if I decide to jump again
golden wings won't grow from the blades in my
back
and no life force will carry me through the sky

No, now I know
manipulated by a trance-like source with mal
intent,
that trusting a charismatic smile
believing in Romeo who waits safely on the
ground
is not enough to make me step off the ledge
so sure that I would fly

Reading fairytales and watching film reels
never could prepare me for this
for only having what seems like myself
to blame for another's careless mistake
for holding my hand out
reaching for an anchor to still my flight

Guided by angels with poor eyesight
unable to travel through the dark

Now, I know, leaping from my windowsill
will surely end my life

-e.m.

Grey (15)

I find comfort in the grey sky above me
in the harrowing winds
in the chaotic movement of the trees
they too, know what it is like!
to be on the verge of a storm
every drop of unpredictable rain threatening an
overpour

I move into my curated home
the place that shelters me as I run away
for what could possibly come after a sky so grey
a wind so cold
surely the sun will not rise
I close my eyes
and whisper a final "goodbye"

-e.m.

Strawberry love (16)

I sang a chorus of desire and admiration
Crafted you sweets to indulge
burning my fingers on melted chocolate
I went down on my knees
but not to pray
and laid down on command
but not to dream
My songs couldn't reach through
the dirt shoved in your ears
My sugar never tasted
with your preference for salt
My obedience and submission
never enough
pinned down
broken down
thrown around
until I had enough

-e.m.

Regret (17)

My pen doesn't run dry
when it comes to you
to the lessons seared into my skin
to the reoccurring dreams
and my prayers to the moon

-e.m.

She's finally (18)

You couldn't wait one more year
You couldn't wait till I could drive my own car

This number so symbolic in time
how did you rob me so blindly
of innocence, once mine

You couldn't wait to pick me up from school
You couldn't wait to take me home

A minor no more
so now you do as you please
not that it seemed to matter before

But I remember
and I regret
the times that I slept in your bed
I thought you were safe
when I should have run far
goddamnit you
you stole a piece of a child's innocent heart

-e.m.

Burning away (19)

I knew I never needed the grass in my lungs
but under my feet
I swore I'd never follow in my father's footsteps
but did so with another substance that too
resulted in defeat
I won't reach down
I won't let the anchors of my fears
keep me on the ground
I will reach up toward all that is good
following the direction of smoke into the sky
to search for what is missing
to not stop until it is found

-e.m.

I Will Feel Better Again (20)

I was done giving in
to the habits my hurt created
I was done seeing the world
in lifeless colors
in empty passing hours
in all that I was not

When my attempts fall short
my world will not end
for I understand
the rise that accompanies the fall
I will feel better again

-e.m.

You Are Not Alone (21)

25

Take a deep breath my friend
I know how it goes
late nights, rough mornings
you are not alone
Take a deep breath my friend
you are fighting
and that is enough
you are not alone
Take a deep breath my friend
for all your darkness
there will be light
you are not alone

-e.m.